Dedicated to all those who work hard to touch the lives of offenders.

TABLE OF CONTENTS

Preface

The practice of the probation and supervision of orders has posed a big challenge to me since I was employed. However it has opened my insights into many social issues. After employment, Probation officers are taken through an induction process to enable them understand the subject matter of Probation practice.

Before and after going for induction, I noted several challenges that got me wondering from that time onwards. I remember that I was guided into how to write a social inquiry report, present the report to court and after that supervise the offenders. When we went for induction, I realized that the profession had attracted people from diverse backgrounds. Some were not lucky as I was to have been guided well into the how of doing of non-custodial sentencing work. From then on I began asking myself several questions: How did the new probation officer find his way through, especially where there was no guidance? Is it always the case there will be somebody to guide in what is expected of a probation officer, what happens if none is present? What about if one went through training and never had a chance of understanding the subject matter of non-custodial service?

These questions prompted me to think about a book that

could act as guide to the newly recruited officers or anybody interested in knowing a little more about non-custodial service. I thought that the workshops and seminars that we have been attending for professional development could be well utilized if the experiences gained could be reflected upon and put in form of a book. I also faced the biggest challenge of not finding anything about non-custodial practice in Kenya from the internet-the main source of my research.

The book was born out of a general curiosity to reflect upon some aspects of non-custodial services. It takes a broad view, but tries also to look at the local Kenyan context. The book takes a general approach not going into the specifics of the practice in Kenya. However, this is rich lacuna for future writings.

The project was also inspired by the director Probation and After Care services Mr Jerim O Oloo who from the first day he addressed us challenged us to contribute positively towards the development of the profession through what we are best at. In all the seminars and forums that we have been taken through, this theme has resonated. The District Probation Officer Tana River whom I have had the chance to work with Mr David Mui encouraged me to think and put the ideas down when he realized I could do it.

Other people who inspired the writing of the book were Steve Wakhu who gave valuable feedback on the manuscript. He told me to ensure that the project and the dream see the light of day. I am grateful to all those who have continued to inspire me and urge me to ensure that the book rolls out of print.

1.0 BACKGROUND:

To develop any profession, it must have a theoretical basis. Such a base distinguishes each profession from the other, provides clarity, forms the basis for development and provides opportunities for critique. Theories not only explain phenomenon, but also interrogates the routine. This has been the field of scholars and researchers, while the real professionals more often have remained in the periphery often going through the rituals of their profession with religious zeal.

As a result, many professionals have missed golden opportunities to express their own critique of theories that inform the basis of what they do on a daily basis. The following enquiry attempts to fill this gap within the non-custodial sentencing in Kenya. Currently, there is an attempt within the department to provide the theoretical foundation of non-custodial sentences. Field staffs are called upon to reflect on what they do and give the practice a professional view. Giving the practice its professional view involves grounding what the practice is all about on some known sociological, philosophical or psychological basis. By so doing, attempts must be made to discover how these fields interact and converge to provide meaning to the non-custodial practice.

The following work is largely based on experiences gained in the field practice and internet research. Field practice has provided the real experience where I have had chance to practice probation work and supervise community service.

The practice of probation in Kenya faces the challenge of availing reflections on the foundations of the practice. It is not likely for instance that one would find a book of "practice of non-custodial service in Kenya". However, great resources abound in form of guidelines, standards and government policy on the practice of non-custodial service. On these policies, laws and guidelines the probation and community services have been in the country since before independence.

We are in the era of information technology. Recorded information is revolutionalizing the way reality is shaped more so because of speed within which information is able to travel from one end of the globe to the other. We cannot be left behind in the non-custodial practice in Kenya. The profession must also take the cue in sharing its best practices in order to improve service delivery.

2.0 OBJECTIVE OF NON-CUSTODIAL SENTENCE PRACTICE

Non-custodial sentencing is a policy decision usually legislated by countries that embrace it. The objectives of the option emanate from the human rights doctrine and the influence of the United Nation. To understand the objectives of non-custodial sentencing it is important to understand the United Nations and the human rights views. These bodies draw heavily from the modern penal debate that places a great value on the human beings beyond the offence committed.

Non-custodial sentencing refers to the punishment meted out on offenders by the criminal justice system that does not include imprisonment or incarceration and the offender pays back by abiding to some set rules, regulations or performs a task that benefits the society. From the onset, the non-custodial sentencing advocates that imprisoning offenders does not reform them neither does it deter them from recidivism. The United Nation has set out guidelines which form the basis for non-custodial sentencing among the member states.

These minimum rules have formed the basis for the design and the implementation of the non-custodial sentences. The rules provides for the consideration of community participation in rehabilitation of the offenders, respect of the inherent rights of the offenders as human beings and emphasis of the realization that penalization does not work to effectively rid the society of crime. Thus, a probation officer who is effectively a non-custodial sentencing officer must embrace these rules. Above all the rules do cover all areas of the non-custodial practice including what he governments should consider in coming up with legislations.

In Kenya, the objective of the non-custodial sentencing is summed up by the probation service motto: Offenders can change. Offenders Can Change focuses on the offender. All efforts and programmes of the department goes towards empowering the offender to change from the offending behavior. It also places a lot of premium on community participation in the changing of the offender. Following the reforms that the country is undertaking in the last few years, the other main objective has been to decongest the penal institutions. This has been due to the realization that it is far much cheaper to rehabilitate the offender while in the community rather than in a penal institution. It has also been appreciated that penalization produces hard core criminals through contamination, enhances social stigmatization and reduces the chances of the offender to get involved in meaningful economic activities.

The probation officer is faced with challenge of getting to understand all the aspects of offending or criminality and then translate the understanding into practical programmes. The department's existence over the years has come up with policies, guidelines and legislation that guide the practice of the profession which often translates the policies into executable programmes. However, newly recruited officers need endeavor to understand non-custodial practice in its theoretical framework too. Just following the rules and guidelines as set out in policy may not be sufficient by itself. For beyond the practice, the practitioner must endeavor to offer constructive critique, offer new insights and document any new experience encountered in the field.

The current world debate does give a lot of emphasis on restorative justice. In its basic form, it aims at enabling the offender to be taken back to the state he/she was in before offending. That state involves enabling the offender to realize that beyond the offence, he/she has a dignity. Restorative justice goes beyond just making the offender pay for the wrongs done, it empowers him/her too to have capacity of refraining from repeat or another offence in future. This encompasses rehabilitation. The non-custodial officer serves best to advance this objective because he is neither a police officer, a legal officer but more of a friend to the offender. If non-custodial program were to achieve its objective, then the officer must fully understand and implement the tenets of restorative justice.

This book therefore aims to introduce the officer to the theoretical framework that guides the practice of non-custodial service from a bird's eye view perspective. The greatest impetus in putting these ideas down is the need to build a link between the theories and practice. Theories inform practice and practice would be routine without ideas that should be constantly evaluated. Practice without answering the "why" of the routine activities leads to underdevelopment. Ironically, there is no better research environment than in the practice.

3.0 THEORETICAL FOUNDATION:

CRIME

Probation and community service falls under the disciples of law, sociology, criminology and psychology. Staffs in the profession are normally trained social scientists. The practice cuts across the above disciplines but is heavily grounded on criminology. Criminology is studied both as aspect of sociology and law. However, historically the practice was not philosophically thought out before inception. In fact, the first probation officer in the world was neither a sociologist, a lawyer nor an intellectual, but a common man who just tried something that has now assumed a professional view.

In this section we are going to take an overview of theoretical framework around the theme of crime. The beginning point is to understand what is crime in the social construct. Sociology has for years tried to understand society in its widest sense. It endeavors to understand the individuals in a social system. Sociology attempts to understand all the aspects of society and explains why the society operates the way it does. From it then, different fields of study and practice have emerged.

Criminology is the study of "how crime is measured, who commits crimes and why, and how society responds. Criminologists look for ways to understand the nature and impact of behavioral and social problems, and ways of alleviating their impact" (Austrarian Institute of Crimonology, 2009) By extension then this introduces the meaning of crime in terms of law, and community reaction to crime. Non-custodial sentencing deals with the subject of crime-the offender or the criminal. This focus draws one's attention to dynamics that are at play in the individual. The main question of exploration at this point is: What causes crime? What is the connection between the criminal and the crime? Can the criminal be held responsible for own criminal behavior? Can crime be cured? Can justice be achieved in the society?

Several theories exist that define crime, explain the crime phenomenon and above all that try to offer the treatment for criminal tendencies. Sociologists attempts to explain why society operates the way it does. We are going to take an overview of some basic sociological ideas and criminological theories.

4.0 SOCIOLOGY, INDIVIDUAL, SOCIETY AND CRIME.

In his book (Inkeles, 1997) defines sociology as "the study of systems of social action and their interrelationships". He suggests that the systems of social action differ in complexity and size. He gives the following as examples of the systems-single social acts, social relationships, organizations and institutions, communities and societies.

This definition is not only comprehensive but offers a good point of departure in the exploration of the subject at hand. Sociology can simply be understood as the study of society in its complex form. Many classical and modern sociologists have labored to define not only the scope but also the subject matter of sociology. Among the notable scholars in this respect are Auguste Compte, Herbert Spencer, Emille Durkheim, MaxWeber who are considered the founders of sociology. These scholars labored to provide the subject matter of sociology as a discipline. Their ideas have formed basis for extensive research and policy formulations. They all agree that sociology must enable us to understand society in its widest scope.

Among the ideas postulated by these early scholars, we are going to zero in on the postulations of Emile Durkheim. Not that they are superior to the rest, but because his ideas offered some greater insights into understanding of crime. Durkheim who was a French sociologist contributed greatly to the field of sociology through two his most important works, *Suicide: A Study in Sociology* and *The Division of Labor in Society* (F. Elwell). He introduced the idea of social facts and asserted that they are "identifiable through the power of external coercion which it exerts or is capable of exerting upon individuals" To him any external power that is able to influence the individual is to be considered a social fact. He continued to argue that through socialization and education individuals come to internalize these constraints which become part of their real selves. He further postulated that human being have dual conscience. On the one hand, there is a part in human beings that propels them to act in a given way but there is the group, or the social consciousness that propels one to follow the group norms and regulations. In this dualism, the group or the social consciousness is supreme and call upon each one to surpass ourselves and act in a given way. But as this is fulfilled the individual feels constrained and sometimes causes friction since the individual is always seeking for what is best for him/her.

To Durkheim, this conflict in dualism brings about what he called a state of anomie. According to the scholar, human being does not integrate properly with the demands of the society. Consequently, the social norms and requirements are not fully obeyed. And "because of the dual nature of human beings this breakdown of moral guidance results in rising rates of deviance, social unrest, unhappiness, and stress" (F. Elwell). In essence then, Durkheim began to offer some insights as to why we have deviance within the society as one of its common systems. He goes on to suggest that desires are the greatest reason why the society has a state of anomie. He notes the "unlimited desires are insatiable by definition and insatiability is rightly considered a sign of morbidity. Being unlimited, they constantly and infinitely surpass the means at their command; they cannot be quenched. Inextinguishable thirst is constantly renewed torture" (F. Elwell)

According to Durkheim, left on his own the individual will only seek that which is self gratifying but that which is beyond him and hence perpetuate the state of anomie. He goes on to suggest that the hope lies in what he calls the collective conscious. He notes, "as there is nothing within an individual which constrains these appetites, they must surely be contained by some force exterior to him, or else they would become insatiable—that is morbid" (F. Elwell)

In essence, Durkheim gave legitimacy for the establishment of formal legal regimes, and gave a seal of approval to those that existed. He noted that human beings accept this collective conscious through such social facts as religion, which does more to reinforce the collective consciousness over the individual.

Thus in Durkheim, we find a logical understanding of our subject of inquiry. He introduces the subject of sociology as the study of social facts and how they are exercised in the individual and how they affect the society. The most important contribution is his admission that human being on his own cannot function as expected partly because of what he called human dualism and partly because of division of labor which alienates individual to seek his/her gratification. Thus he grapples with the question: what is crime? He prefers not to call it crime though, but instead prefers to use the word anomie. In his explanation of crime he did research on why there was increased suicide cases, he concluded suicide was likely to occur where the social cohesion bond was weak.

Alex Inkeles offers an introduction to some of these social facts and does explore conformity, variance and deviance as fundamental social processes. He begins by noting that these processes in a society ensure that people meet their social roles and obligations. He defines conformity as "doing what one is expected to do" (Inkeles, 1997). Conformity is enhanced by the concepts of reward and punishment. These rewards and punishments are enforced by the groups and society to which the individual belongs. Society sanctions favorably those who conform and metes out negative sanctions to those who do not. But this arrangement presupposes that society must police each individual in order to enhance conformity. He argues that each individual needs to be internally motivated to ensure conformity to the social roles. Sociologists explain social deviance based on this background.

Social deviance "arises when the departure from accepted norms involves action about which the community feels strongly, so strongly as to adopt sanctions to prevent or otherwise control the deviant behavior" (Inkeles, 1997) Debate on the causes of social deviance is varied and extensive. The definition by Inkeles falls short of explaining all the actions that the society sanctions either negatively or positively. However it does to some extent offer some probable understanding of the sources of what social construct of crime is. The author does agree that social deviance is an important subject matter of sociologists, implying that it cannot be wished away and probably it has some utility value. At any one given time society does define what it sanctions favorably or negatively through its norms, traditions, religion and the general socialization process. The more strong these traditions and norms are the more conspicuous will be social deviance.

5.0 CRIMINOLOGY THEORIES

The foregoing debate has introduced some of the sociological thinking as much as it relates to crime. But crime is studied in its own field-criminology. Although this may be the case, there are non-custodial enforcement officers who have not had a chance to study criminology, yet the knowledge is essential for effective practice. Understanding criminology requires one to have exposure to postulations about human behavior. It requires one to understand how the human being come to make the decision that he/she makes on a daily life. Such understanding should not only be viewed on its own but also relative to the social environment into which one belongs. Scholars and researchers have delved into this matter and put forward their thoughts.

5.1 Cognitive Theory

Criminology theories try to answer some basic questions: What is crime? How are we to understand crime? We begin our browse by exploring the cognitive theories. Cognitive theories try to explain behavior in general. "The social cognitive theory explains how people acquire and maintain certain behavioral patterns, while also providing the basis for intervention strategies" (Twente University) Cognitive theories do provide for the following basic assumptions:

❖ *That environment affects how someone*

behaves:

> Social cognitive theorist visualize environment as both social and physical. Social environment include family background, the peer groups, work environment. Simply the environment where an individual interacts with others or is influenced by other individuals.

❖ *Situation affect how people behave*: Situation is a person's perception of the lace, time, physical features and activity. It is the way the individual interprets the environment.

❖ *People in one's life do also determine behavior.*

Cognitive theories do indicate that the three factors environment, situation and people do influence each other all the time and hence determine how one behaves. The factors role is to provide mental construct of decision arrived at and hence the actions emanating from those decisions. But behavior can also be learnt. When the individual watches the environment, he/she can learn a pattern of behavior.

There are some important concepts that must be considered when referring to the cognitive theories. They are:

Environment: Factors physically external to the person; Provides opportunities and social support

Situation: Perception of the environment; correct misperceptions and promote healthful forms

Behavioral capability: Knowledge and skill to perform a given behavior; promote mastery learning through skills training

Expectations: Anticipatory outcomes of a behavior; Model positive outcomes of healthful behavior

Expectancies: The values that the person places on a given outcome, incentives; Present outcomes of change that have functional meaning

Self-control: Personal regulation of goal-directed behavior or performance; Provide opportunities for self-monitoring, goal setting, problem solving, and self-reward *Observational learning:* Behavioral acquisition that occurs by watching the actions and outcomes of others" behavior; Include credible role models of the targeted behavior *Reinforcements:* Responses to a person's behavior that increase or decrease the likelihood of reoccurrence; Promote self-initiated rewards and incentives

Self-efficacy: The person's confidence in performing a particular behavior; Approach behavioral change in small steps to ensure success.

Emotional coping responses: Strategies or tactics that are used by a person to deal with emotional stimuli; provide training in problem solving and stress management *Reciprocal determinism:* The dynamic interaction of the person, the behavior, and the environment in which the behavior is performed; consider multiple avenues to behavioral change, including environmental, skill, and personal change. (Twente University)

Thus a certain behavior in human beings could be planned or spontaneous. Where planned, the individual is motivated by some expectations that are deemed to have utility value. The utility or the functionality of the expected behavior determine how much the individual repeats the behavior or shuns it all together. If the outcome of the behavior is as expected, the possibility of reoccurrence of the same increases hence forming a behavioral pattern that become manifest and one that come to be associated with a certain individual. Where the expectations may not be as planned, the individual learns how to deal with the failures or eventual successes and this is exhibited through the emotional manifestation of the resultant outcomes. Reciprocal determinism implies to the non-static nature of the individual, the exhibited behavior and the environment that one lives in. The three factors are not passive in any exhibited behavior, but dynamically affect each other. In evaluating a certain behavior, analysis using this theory presupposes that the individual behavior cannot be viewed in isolation-rather it is a product of a system. A spontaneous behavior may fail to follow the logical process as outlined, but does bear the some elements. The key factor is that cognitive theorists do agree that behavior emanates from a rational process but could be informed by the environment and the individual innate factors too.

Is crime to be viewed as a behavior? Answered affirmatively one will then pose the question, can cognitive theory help us to explain it. According to cognitive theory if crime is a behavior, then the individual is not entirely to blame. Rather, one should consider both the social and physical environment to understand it. To the non-custodial officer, this could be worth consideration. But the difficulty in using this model alone comes when one tries to draw the boundary between the individual's responsibility towards crime and the role of the environment. How far should the environment be viewed to influence one to perform a crime or to become a habitual criminal? To what extent should the individual take responsibility of own behavior?

5.2 Choice Theory:

This theory is summarized as follows:
- o *people freely choose* all their behavior; that motives such as greed, revenge, need, anger, lust, jealousy, thrill-seeking, and vanity are just expressions of free will or at least expressions of personal choice, conclusion, or decision making that people have made;
- o *choices can be controlled* by fear of punishment; because people weigh the potential benefits and consequences of crime, some people concluding that the risk of

punishment is worth the satisfaction of crime; and

- ○ *the more certain, swift, and severe the punishment*, the greater is its ability to control criminal behavior, especially if the punishment is fair and serves some rational and legitimate purpose (a tangible incentive to obey the law) (Twente University)

As its name suggest this group of theories place the burden of crime commission on the individual. They emphasize that the individual engages in a cost benefit analysis before committing a crime. If the cost of committing a crime (read punishment or negative sanctions) is higher, the individual is likely to shun the action but if the benefit is greater, the individual is likely to repeat the behavior. The theorists argue that the surety of punishment, its timeliness and its magnitude determine whether a behavior will be repeated or avoided. Its advocates do not favor rehabilitation but argue that rehabilitation is a waste of time.

Choice theories do suggest that individuals do rationalize about crime commission. That for a crime to occur three things must present- potential offender, suitable targets and incapable, unwilling or absent guardians. The potential offender chooses a suitable target to commit a crime. The absence of anyone, or authority to deter him/her to commit the crime motivates him/her to commit it. Accordingly, any crime committed is to be viewed as a result of a rational process that the offender undergoes. This rationalization process makes it possible to practice deterrence, detection and delaying of the commission of crime.

Deterrence of crime is the restraint from committing a crime. Deterrence can be general or specific. Deterrence works under the following assumptions:
1) the vast majority of potential law breakers are sane/rational thinking persons;
(2) the amount of crime in society should equal the opportunities perceived by criminals; and
(3) the greater the costs & losses, the lower the willingness to engage in crime & vice versa (i.e., cost and willingness are inversely related). Deterrence is thought to be effective if the certainty/probability of getting caught is directly related to the severity of punishment; i.e.,

Certainty <=> punishment severity; and if the punishment is quick; i.e., punishment => quick. (National Insitute of Justice)

For the non-custodial service officer, this enables him/her understand what programs to put in place to achieve the

objective. The core reasoning behind the non-custodial sentencing is enhancing deterrence from the commission of crime. The crime commission is done and enhanced by the rationalizing individual but deterrence is enhanced by the social systems-laws, norms, and community at large. Deterrence could be general-one that is capable of deterring others would be offenders from offending, or specific-one which is capable of reducing recidivism. Marginal deterrence occur when petty offences attract same punishment as serious offences. The effect of marginal deterrence is to make the offender commit the offence that would attract the severest punishment.

5.4 Anthropological Theory

This is the old school of thought that explain crime from anthropological standpoint. Its advocates argue that it is possible to know a criminal by examining the physical features of a potential offender. Its main proponents believe that criminals are primitive human beings whose features are close those of monkeys and chimpanzees. Cesare Lombrosso the pioneer of anthropological criminal came up with a list of features that he thought described criminals. That an individual who has the following features was likely to engage in crime:

- Unusually short or tall height
- Small head, but large face
- Small and sloping forehead
- Receeding hairline

- Wrinkles on forehead and face
- Large sinus cavities or bumpy face

- Large, protruding ears
- Bumps on head, particularly the Destructiveness Center above left ear
- Protuberances (bumps) on head, in back of head and around ear
- High cheek bones
- Bushy eyebrows, tending to meet across nose
- Large eyesockets, but deepset eyes
- Beaked nose (up or down) or flat nose
- Strong jawline
- Fleshy lips, but thin upper lip
- Mighty incisors, abnormal teeth
- Small or weak chin
- Thin neck
- Sloping shoulders, but large chest
- Long arms
- Pointy or snubbed fingers or toes
- Tatoos on body (Abretcht)

Those who followed his thoughts went further to develop anthropological features of juveniles likely to be involved in crime. Notable among them was William Sheldon (1899-1977), who developed a relationship between the physical features and temperaments. He came up with the following classification:

- *Endomorphic* -- tendency to put on fat, soft roundness of body, short tapering limbs, small bones, velvety skin; *viscerotonic* temperament, relaxed, comfortable person, loves luxury, an extrovert.

- *Mesomorphic* -- predominance of muscles, bone, and motor organs, large trunk, heavy chest, large wrist and hands, lean rectangular outline; *somotonic* or Dionysian temperament, active, assertive, aggressive, unrestrained.
- *Ectomorphic* -- predominance of skin, lean, fragile, delicate body, small bones, droppy shoulders, small face, sharp nose, fine hair; *cerebrotonic* temperament, sensitive, distractible, insomnia, skin troubles, allergies

William came up with a scale of numbers 1-7 to indicate the dominance of each of the above features in a person. Such as 7-1-4, which would mean more of endomorphic features, little mesomorphic and an average of ectomorphic features. He used the scale to map out delinquency among juveniles and concluded juveniles with 3-5-2 somatype were likely to be delinquent. For sometime, anthropological criminology was widely used and became the basis on which the criminals are photographed to determine the prominence of anthropological features that were common among criminals or inmates.

The importance of this theoretical understanding is that it brings out the human condition, human nature, human impulses, human bodies, and how humanity always seem to be creating rules and regulations in our communities that reflect those basic things. And because people are diverse, and it is important to study how they get along, with all their different appearances, different languages, and different ways of life. Anthropological criminology links the offender to own humanity in totality and asserts that maybe we could understand crime by focusing on the humanness of an individual.

5.5 Mental Deficiency Theory

This theory links crime to mental capability. It asserts that low intelligence among individuals can be used to understand crime. People with low intelligence are considered as knowing little and do not appreciate the meaning of law, hence are liable to committing crime. Such people, criminologists believe are easily duped into committing crimes as accomplices. There are four ways a person with low intelligence can be used to commit crime, by being duped; by sheer folly; by inability to understand; and by attempting to provide for self (Tibetts & Craig, 2010) This kind of theory exonerates the individual from the criminal tendency. It further presupposes that all crime is driven by some underdeveloped mental faculties.

One criminologist has gone ahead to suggest that this folly in an individual assumes three patterns: mistuning, entrenchment, and under management.

Mistuning he explains has to do with wrong timing and intensity towards build up emotions. Thus a person who is short tempered due to anger is mistuned. He attributes the loss of temper to low intelligence that fails to control the build of emotions towards the cause of anger. Entrenchment occurs when an individual becomes totally absorbed in trying to complete a task. Where unfinished cognitive tasks tend to linger and take up valuable space in our memory until those tasks are resolved. The theorists suggest that people with low intelligence are then likely to engage in crime as their actions are not fully processed by the cognitive mind. Under management on the other hand is the failure to manage the present as a result of past excitement that has prolonged for long. Acting foolishly can then lead one to commit a crime whether knowingly or not.

For the non-custodial service officers, the issue is to determine to what extent can this theory assist in understanding how crime can be understood. For instance, do all criminals have low intellect?

5.6 Biological Theory

This theory asserts that some criminal behavior is triggered by the some bodily organs. The theory is also known as psychobiological theory. Its main contribution to understanding crime is its assertion that crime can be linked to hormones, neurotransmitters and vitamins present in a human body. According to this theory, hormones produced by endocrine glands, brain, gastrointestinal organs, sex organs, the kidney, the heart, the pineal glands and the hair do exert a strong influence on behavior. They induce the brain to cause people to behave in certain way in reaction to the environmental stimuli. It continues to assert that "hormones not only influence reactive or conscious behavior after environmental cues, but they also influence anticipatory or unconscious behavior (by knowing what the body needs beforehand, hormones make a person think they want something before they see it) (Tibetts & Craig, 2010) It therefore means to understand crime, one must try to understand what hormones triggered the criminal activity.

Proponents of this theory suggest that key component of this theory is how it explains the central motive state or simply desire. They assert that hormonal reactions produce desires that are appetitive (that trigger searching) and a consummatory (fulfilling) phases. The interplay of these desires in the human psychology then produce certain behavioral patterns. A notable point is that although individuals by themselves can probably generate the appetitive phase of a hormonal reaction, they need the hormonal reactions of others (pheromones) or additional environmental stimuli to generate the consummatory phase The net effect of this fact is that if a person initiates a certain desire, the desire must be translated into a form of activity that describes a behavior. It then implies that it is possible that crime arises out of some desires that may not be approved by the society, hence labeled as crime.

Proponents of the theory have developed the following schemata to show how hormones influence behavior:

Endocrine gland:	Hormone released:	Behavior influenced
Pituitary (anterior lobe)	Growth hormone, Prolactin, ACTH, LH, TSH, FSH	Food preference, brooding, parenting, quiescence
Pituitary (posterior lobe)	Arginine vosopressin, Oxytocin, Endorphins, Enkephalins	Hunger, attachment behavior, sexual behavior, pain, aggression
Pineal	Melatonin	Sleepiness
Thyroid	Thyroxine, Calcitonin	Nervousness
Parathyroid	Parathyroid hormone	Sickness, immune system
Heart factor	Atrial	Water/sodium ingestion

Kidney	Renin	Hunger
Skin	Vitamin D	Mood, melancholy
Liver/lung	Preangiostensin, Angiotensin	Thirst, hunger
Pancreas	Insulin, Glucagon	Food satiety
Stomach/intestines	Cholecystokinin, Peptides, Bombesin, Somatostatin	Food satiety
Gonads (ovary)	Estrogen, Progesterone	Female sex drive, aggression, territoriality
Gonads (testis)	Testosterone, Substance P	Male sex drive, pain

Lymphocytes   Cytokines

Sleepiness   (Source:

www.apsu.edu/oconnort/crim/crimtheory)

In explaining criminal behavior, theorists and biologists focus more on the effects of testosterone and some androgens. Researchers on this field have linked their dominant presence to reduced social integration which triggers deviance. For instance, women are thought to be more irritable when some of these hormones are dominant. Some of the seasonal disorders have been explained using this theory also.

Apart from the hormones, the other component of the biological theory is the effect of the neurotransmitters. Neurotransmitters are chemicals that allow the transmission of electrical impulses in the brain and main ways the brain uses to process information. Neurotransmitters are involved principally in the central nervous system and are responsible for cognitive functioning of the brain. In studying criminology, neurotransmitters are used to explain the antisocial behavior. It is thought that things like alcohol and drugs   affect the   neurotransmitter levels. Neurotransmitters are hereditary but can significantly be altered by use of drugs, stress and by altitude. They affect the cognitive functioning of the brain thereby impairing the sense of judgment.

Neurotransmitter:	Behavior affected:
Serotonin (vitamin Tryptophan)	Pain reduction, aggression
Dopamine (vitamin Tyrosine)	Pleasure enhancement, schizophrenia
Norepinephrine/Epinephrine	Moods, feeling states
Acetylcholine (vitamin Choline)	Moods, feeling states

Source: www.apsu.edu/oconnort/crim/crimtheory)

"Serotonin is probably the most important neurotransmitter in criminology. As stated previously, antisocial people have lower levels of serotonin. This may be either genetic or environmental, because neurotransmitter balances are constantly changing as memories are stored in the brain. Every new memory permanently changes the neural pathway structure, thus creating the opportunities for neurotransmitter imbalances. People who are genetically endowed with lower serotonin levels ("born antisocials") may therefore "grow out of it," and likewise, someone who is born with normal serotonin levels may develop an antisocial personality (what is called "reduced serotonergic activity" or a "serotonin uptake problem"). Reduced serotonic activity and crime is one of the strongest connections in bio-psychological criminology" (Tibetts & Craig, 2010)

The debate here is that for you to understand crime, there must be a way of determining the levels of neurotransmitters in the brain to draw a link to the exhibited antisocial behavior. Inversely, it implies that one can explain a certain behavior by referring to the levels of specific transmitters as the plausible explanation. For instance, some research suggest that criminals have lower rate of skin conductance (slow rate of conducting electrical currents from the skin to the brain). The presence of such scenario reduces the criminal's perception of fear. The effect of this is to cause the dysfunctioning of the frontal lobe. Research has shown that there's evidence to suggest that frontal lobe dysfunction may characterize violent offenders while temporal lobe dysfunction may characterize sex offender.

Vitamin deficiencies/dependencies have been thought to influence the criminal tendencies within individuals. Vitamin deficiencies cause low intelligence (IQ) causing mental impairment and low immune systems. Vitamin dependency works different. Each person is born with required vitamins. Consumption of vitamins that leads to dependency act the same way toxicity works in the body or drugs overdose. They trigger behavior associated with crime.

5.7 Developmental and Moral Developmental Theory

Developmental theories explain the different stages of development from birth to adulthood. Moral development theories explain the psychological disposition in the different stages of development. As far as crime is concerned, developmental theories hold that criminal tendencies is controlled by inherent and inborn traits, they are determinate. As such, it is possible to identify the criminal traits of individuals by tracing the development of criminality with the stages of development. On the other hand, moral development holds that criminal behavior is dynamic and is influenced by the individual and social experiences. Moral development theories in attempting to explain criminality asserts that it can be caused by everything in a particular stage. For instance, it suggests that adolescence is the cause of delinquency and crime among adolescents.

Developmental theories are ideal for explaining the criminality among the adolescents and bring out the following themes to be considered when dealing with the adolescents:

- **Self-definition** -- a concern for finding one's "real" self, a concern for habit formation, and little unstructured time to deal with these concerns, hence, a constant state of urgency.
- **Estrangement and Omnipotentiality** estrangement takes the form of feeling like a marginal member of society, with unrealistic mobility aspirations and intense job anxieties. Omnipotentiality is the feeling of absolute freedom, a reveling in all the pure possibilities that the future may hold. For many, the "car" becomes a symbol for this.
- **Refusal of Socialization**--- critical if not rebellious stance at continued efforts to instruct, educate, or train for society's purposes. There's a feeling of always being

under observation by a critical audience of all adult socializing agent

- **Celebration of Youth Culture** -- a rebellious sense of solidarity based on the perceived sharing of fads, fashions, and styles by others in the same age group or generation; intense age-consciousness.

- **Stasis as Death** -- stasis means "standing still" or being in a rut, and this is avoided and despised at all costs. There's an irrational devotion to change, to putting oneself through changes merely for the sake of change. It takes two forms: a need to move (geographic restlessness); and a need to be moved (experimentation with states of consciousness).

- **Physical Obsession** -- there's an obsessiveness or inadmissible sense of shame over uncontrollable physical changes, like sex fantasies, body weight and contours, dietary habits, the outgrowing of clothing, outbreaks of acne, etc.

When dealing with a delinquent youth it is thus important to trace how these themes come into play. By discovering how the themes interplay at various point in the adolescents' life, the proponents think that it is possible to discover the criminogenic needs. Once the criminogenic needs are traced, then it may be possible to come up with possible intervention strategies. Through the practice of non-custodial sentencing options, then it is important to know whether these theoretical postulation hold.

5.8 Psychopathy Theory

This theory is used to explain crime in habitual (for lack of a better term) criminals. It refers to those who consistently violate the rights of others and still make fun about it. Simply put, the criminals referred in this theory will commit a very serious and nasty crime and their conscious will not be pricked and worst of all, they will make fun about it. To them, there is no sense of guilt or being mistreated. Psychopaths have been defined as "as a constellation of affective, interpersonal, and behavioral characteristics including egocentricity; impulsivity; irresponsibility; shallow emotions; lack of empathy, guilt, or remorse; pathological lying; manipulativeness; and the persistent violation of social norms and expectations" (Tibetts & Craig, 2010)

In most cases, the crimes committed by these criminals are highly negatively sanctioned by the society but those who commit them will continue to commit them. Psychopathy is term commonly used in psychology and it"s important to point out that there is an axiom that "most psychopaths are antisocial personalities, but not all antisocial-personalities are psychopaths" (Tibetts & Craig, 2010)
This is so because the antisocial personalities so described are based on their behaviors that have a social

bearing while psychopaths behavior may be attributed to some aspects of affective or interpersonal characteristics. While the sociopaths may one day grow out of their sociopathic behavior, the psychopaths do not come out of their obsessions. They will leave it for a while but will easily revert back-recidivistic. Psychopaths, instead of seeing the harm committed, they intellectualize about it. Common psychopathic traits are-

- "Glib and superficial charm;
- Grandiose sense of self-worth;
- Need for stimulation;
- Pathological lying;
- Conning and manipulativeness;
- Lack of remorse or guilt;
- Shallow affect;
- Callousness and lack of empathy;
- Parasitic lifestyle;
- Poor behavioral controls;
- Promiscuous sexual behavior;
- Early behavior problems;
- Lack of realistic, long-term goals;
- Impulsivity;
- Irresponsibility;
- Failure to accept responsibility for own actions;
- Many short-term marital relationships;
- Juvenile delinquency;
- Revocation of conditional release;
- Criminal versatility"

Psychopaths are classified in four subgroups:

- **Distempered psychopaths** are the kind that seems to fly into a rage or frenzy more easily and more often than other subtypes. Their frenzy will resemble an epileptic fit. They are also usually men with incredibly strong sex drives, capable of astonishing feats of sexual energy, and seemingly obsessed by sexual urges during a large part of their waking lives. Powerful cravings also seem to characterize them, as in drug addiction, kleptomania, pedophilia, any illicit or illegal indulgence. They like the endorphin "high" or "rush" off of excitement and risk-taking. The serial-rapist-murderer known as the Boston Strangler was such a psychopath.
- **Charismatic psychopaths** are charming, attractive liars. They are usually gifted at some talent or another, and they use it to their advantage in manipulating others. They are usually fast-talkers, and possess an almost demonic ability to persuade others out of everything they own, even their lives. Leaders of religious sects or cults, for example, might be psychopaths if they lead their followers to their deaths. This subtype often comes to believe in their own fictions. They are irresistible.
- **Primary psychopaths do** not respond to punishment, apprehension, stress, or disapproval. They seem to be able to inhibit their antisocial impulses most of the time, not

because of conscience, but because it suits their purpose at the time. Words do not seem to have the same meaning for them as they do for us. In fact, it's unclear if they even grasp the meaning of their own words, a condition that Cleckley called "semantic aphasia." They don't follow any life plan, and it seems as if they are incapable of experiencing any genuine emotion.

- **Secondary psychopaths** are risk-takers, but are also more likely to be stress-reactive, worriers, and guilt-prone. They expose themselves to more stress than the average person, but they are as vulnerable to stress as the average person. They are daring, adventurous, unconventional people who began playing by their own rules early in life. They are strongly driven by a desire to escape or avoid pain, but are unable to resist temptation. As their anxiety increases toward some forbidden object, so does their attraction to it. They live their lives by the lure of temptation.

On the other hand sociopathy is associated with conscience. Sociopaths are those who will care less about others and only care about fulfilling their own egocentric desires. It is thought to result out of poor parenting-where the parent was not present or where present was grossly
incapable of socializing such a person. It takes any

three of the following characters to describe a sociopath:

- Egocentricy;
- Callousness;
- Impulsivity;
- Conscience defect;
- Exaggerated sexuality;
- Excessive boasting;
- Risk taking;
- Inability to resist temptation;
- Antagonistic, deprecating attitude toward the opposite sex;
- Lack of interest in bonding with a mate

There are four known sub-types of sociopaths as follows:

- **Common sociopaths**: They are ashamed by those things that would shame you. They enjoy bending or breaking all rules. They don"t have a sense of guilt as you do. "Nevertheless, they seem genuinely happy with their lives, unburdened by any sense of negative self-worth or the fact that they have not been a functional, contributing member of society"
- **Alienated sociopaths**: They have never developed ability to love, or express empathy. They are more concerned about their pets, personal artifacts or their own bodies. They feel cheated by the society and hence care less about it. They are chronic complainers and above all they would not mind the society being

destroyed apart from them.

- **Aggressive sociopaths:** They derive joy in harming others. They like to hurt, terrorize, frighten and bully others. "They do it for a sense of power and control, and will often only drop subtle hints about what they are up to"[35] They will always get their way and will do sadistic things in their spare time. If opposed to achieve their goals they are vindictive in their response.
- **Dyssocial sociopaths**: They subscribe to sub-cultures that are counter to the popular cultures. They are capable of following them with intense passion but will not agree that they willingly chose to belong to such sub-cultures.

5.9 Anti Personality Theory

Unlike sociopathy, and to the extreme psychopathy, antisocial personality disorder affects very normal people. Once in a while a well socialized person will suffer from the condition-antisocial personality disorder. "The main characteristic of it is a complete and utter disregard for the rights of others and the rules of society. They seldom show anxiety and don't feel guilt." (Tibetts & Craig, 2010) However, this disregard of the others is not permanent, but fades away with time. The following are some of the identified features of persons suffering from anti-social personality disorder:

1. Failure to conform to social norms;
2. Deceitfulness, manipulativeness;
3. Impulsivity, failure to plan ahead;
4. Irritability, aggressiveness;
5. Reckless disregard for the safety of self or others;
6. Consistent irresponsibility;
7. Lack of remorse after having hurt, mistreated, or stolen from another person

The important note is that these features can manifest in any normal individual. It can explain why the individual committed a certain crime. In the justification of their actions, those suffering from this disorder may site reasons that comprise of the following traits: Sense of entitlement; Unremorseful; Apathetic to others; Unconscionable behavior; Blameful of others; Manipulative and conning; Affectively cold; Disparate understanding; Socially irresponsible; Disregardful of obligations; Nonconforming to norms; Irresponsible (Twente University) Thus one suffering from this condition may have failed to conform to certain social norms because he is entitled to his own opinion. Further probing may show that he might have stolen for instance because he thought he was the one entitled to have whatever was stolen.

5.10 Poverty Theory

This theory bases its argument on the idea of economic differentiation as the cause of crime. Its proponents argue that, social stratification is aggravated by the economic differentiation. It argues that social stratification is usually based on education, occupation and income. Crime arises out of the personal interpretation of equity of economic resources of the social strata. This assessment is influenced by analysis of sociocultural environment and how it relates to the psychological interpretation. If this interpretation is thought to bring inequity, there are attempts put in place to try and address it. This then explains why property crimes occur. Criminals will justify their actions as motivated by the perceived inequality. Proponents of this theory do suggest that there will be more crime where the social stratification is pronounced and where it leads to gross alienation of some members of society from the means of economic empowerment.

5.12 Social Disorganization Theory

This theory explains the sources of crime to be the failure of the social institutions such as education system, governance systems among others. As they fail, subcultures form that eventually breed crime. Thus disorganization refers to the communities' inability to understand how these sub-cultures form and develop to the extent they replace normal social organization. It has the following basic assumptions:

1. Crime and delinquency are caused primarily by social factors (*environmental determinism*)

2. The facts speak imperfectly for themselves, but better if fitted into theory (*positivism*)

3. Official statistics are OK, but fieldwork is better (*acceptance of official arrest data*)

4. The city is a perfect natural laboratory (*cities reflect society as a whole*)

5. Components of social structure are unstable (conflict, anomie, social disorganization; conflict or anomie if talking about political economy or society; social disorganization if talking about cities and neighborhoods)

6. Instabilities and their effects are worse for the lower classes (*lower class crime focus*)

7. Human nature is basically good (*social ability thesis*) but subject to vulnerability and inability to resist temptation.

5.13 Strain Theory

Simply put, crime according to strain theories is likely to result when the normal functioning of the social system is disrupted or inhibited from functioning normally. "Strain theories do a good job in providing structural-functional explanations, and there's some of it in conflict theory and many other approaches too. A purely structural explanation ("how things work") locates a process, event, or factor within a larger structure by emphasizing locations, interdependencies, distances or relations among positions in that structure" (Tibetts & Craig, 2010)This theory borrows heavily from the writings of Emile Durkheim on the causes of crime based on division of labour. The theory suggest that when the society becomes more complicated due to some facts such as division of labor, there is likely to be strain on the social systems which might breed crime. Thus factors causing these disruptions are seen as aggravating crime since individuals will be propelled to find ways of overcoming the strain.

Broadly, strain theories are perpetuated by interrelationship between education, opportunity and occupation. When the education system does not result to better opportunities for economic empowerment, strain may arise and likewise when less education leads to more opportunity then strain might arise. Crime may arise as a reaction to this status. Some proponents of the theory do suggest that this becomes the ideal situation to perpetuate the means justifies the end kind of operation. This leads to development of some adaptations to be able to maintain the structural functionality of the social system. The following is a typology of this adaptations modes as brought out by Merton:

Conformity

Merton recognized conformity as the most common type of the five modes. During this mode, people strive to obtain success by the most pure conventional means available.

Innovation

During innovation, Merton identified a miniscule, but substantial change in the perspective of the people whose mode is still in conformity and that of whom has shifted to innovation. The people continue to seek success; however by innovation they strive to obtain the success by taking advantage of illegal goals available to them in place of less promising conventional means in order to attain success.

Rebellion

Merton suggested that by the time people reach the mode of rebellion, they have completely rejected the story that everybody in society can achieve success and have loomed into a rebellious state. They neither trust the valued cultural ends nor the legitimate societal means used to reach success. Instead, these people replace such ideas with irrational objectives to include the violent overthrow of the system altogether.

Retreatism

Identified by Merton as the escapist response of the five modes, retreatism occurs when people become practically dropouts of society. They give up all goals and efforts to achieve success because they view it as an impractical, impossible, almost imaginary, and irrational possibility. Merton attributes this mode as the one to which drug addicts, alcoholics, vagrants, and the severely mental ill function because their reactions to not being able to obtain success by legitimate means represses them from society.

Ritualism

During ritualism, the final mode, people realize that they have no real opportunity to advance in society and accept the little relevance that they have. It is in this mode that people concentrate on retaining what little they possibly gained or still have in place of concentrating on a higher yield of success. They return to adhering to conventional norms in hopes of maintaining the few possessions or possible gains that they have attained. For many members of the urban lower socioeconomic populous and disadvantaged minorities this period of short-lived and slightly increased gains takes nearly a lifetime to obtain and to recognize its worth in a modern industrial society. (Tibetts & Craig, 2010)

Frustration is another component used to expound strain theory. It states losers in a competition experience strong feelings of frustration or depravation. The competition may be for education, opportunities or resources. While the losers may accept their loss and do nothing about it, some are likely to result to crime. Thus, strain theory using this line of thought envisages a society where there is no competition that marginalizes others. It envisages a fairly egalitarian society. Frustration may be used to trace crime among the repeat offenders and those in lower social class.

Other ways that strain theory try to understand behavior is through the view that deviant association has its own value. Membership to a deviant group does well to legitimize the actions of the group, even though abhorred by the society. It also asserts that, strain may result out of emotional problems. It may arise out of the failure to achieve positively valued goals, removal of positively valued stimuli or due to confrontation with negative stimuli.

5.14 Learning Theory

In its summarized form, this theory asserts that crime is a result of the socialization process. That crime is influenced by the various socialization process players. Thus, external environment in which a person is socialized does make the person to acquire the criminal tendencies. Unlike the biological deterministic theory that asserts that criminal traits are in born, learning theories blame the environment in which the criminal grows up. Learning takes some of the following forms:

- **Association**: When a person associates another who is prone to commit crime, chances are that he/she too will commit crime. Further if the results of the criminal acts are associated with positive values, then crime can and does occur. The following is summary of the association tenets as put forward by some criminologists:
    - Criminal behavior is learned....
    - Criminal behavior is learned in interaction with others in a process of communication....
    - Learning criminal behavior occurs within primary groups (family, friends, peers, their most intimate, personal companions)
    - Learning criminal behavior involves learning the techniques, motives, drives, rationalizations, and attitudes....

    - The specific direction of motives and attitudes is learned from definitions of the legal codes as favorable or unfavorable....
    - A person becomes a criminal when there is an excess of definitions favorable to violation of law over definitions unfavorable to violation of law (differential association)

- Differential associations vary in frequency, duration, priority, and intensity (frequent contacts, long contacts, age at first contact, important or prestigious contacts)
- The process of learning criminal behavior involves all the mechanisms involved in any other learning....
- Although criminal behavior is an expression of general needs and attitudes, criminal behavior and motives are not explained nor excused by the same needs and attitudes

- **Imitation**: This has to do with copying. Some criminologists argue that crime begins as a fashion and later becomes a custom. New crimes for instance do not begin as crimes but as fashion which only later turn out to be undesirable.
- **Reinforcement:** Reinforcement states that after people learn behavior, they learn to reap the benefits of the actual or expected behavior. Thus behavior has highly anticipated outcomes are more repeated. The mental interpretation of the past rewards reinforces the behavior. The following seven steps are followed to reinforce behavior:
  - ❖ Criminal behavior is learned through conditioning or imitation.
  - ❖ Criminal behavior is learned both in

nonsocial reinforcing situations or nonsocial discriminative situations and thru social interaction.

- ❖ The principal components of learning occur in groups.
- ❖ Learning depends on available reinforcement contingencies.
- ❖ The type and frequency of learning depends on the norms by which these reinforcers are applied.
- ❖ Criminal behavior is a function of norms which are discriminative for criminal behavior.
- ❖ The strength of criminal behavior depends upon its reinforcement

Thus to understand criminality is to understand how social learning is reinforced in the criminal psychological disposition. Psychological disposition may take the following forms:

- ❖ Neutralization: This is an admission that criminal are not hopelessly bad people. It asserts that criminals too have the good side of their personality and only drift in crime once in a while. However, when often driven to crime, criminals may use this as an escape route. They escape bearing the responsibility of what is conventionally expected behavior using the following techniques:
- ❖ Denial of responsibility -- It's not my fault; I didn't have a choice
- ❖ Denial of injury -- It's no big deal; They have

too much money

- ❖ Denial of victim -- They had it coming; They had a bad attitude
- ❖ Condemnation of the condemners -- Everybody does it; Why me?
- ❖ Appeal to higher loyalties -- Only cowards back down; protecting[43]

What is important to note on this theory is that it is commonly used to explain the sources of delinquency among youth. Adherents of this theory do suggest that delinquency is not inborn, but rather acquired as the youth grows up.

5.15 Control Theory

This theory explores the reasons why people do not commit crimes. Factors such as the religion, social bonding and the family impact have been researched and there are elements that they do determine the propensity to commit crime. What is important here is that this theory addresses the question of why don't people commit crime? The interesting fact about is that the probation officer would be called upon to see whether this hold. For instance does it imply that those who commit crime do not subscribe to any form of religion? Or, does the level of religious affiliation determine the commission of crime.

5.16 Labeling Theory

Labeling theory asserts that criminal act is so depending on the meaning attached to it. Thus, what could be criminal to one, could actually be labeled as non-criminal by another. It asserts that crime is based on the situation and that there is no universal definition of crime. Criminality of a crime depends on how the criminal interprets the act of crime.

5.17 Conflict Theory

This is a product of Marxist ideologies. It holds that society is not held together by consensus but rather by competing and conflicting values and interests. It implies that those who are weak and cannot access the means of production in a capitalistic state tend to aggravate crime. According to this theory, possession of power determines who can compete better and hence can advance his interests more. This theory is heavily influenced by the Marxist ideas on the nature of man and his ideas on epistemology. For Marx, human beings are not completely evolved but are still evolving to date. Due to their inadequacies they try to explain themselves by reference to higher loyalties. It therefore means, to explain crime as result of socialization or social functionalism does not hold since human beings are constantly improving themselves. Conflict theorists following this line hold that conflict between capitalism and communism, between legislation and real life are main causes of crime. The conflict between the poor and the rich breed crime, not because such criminals were not properly socialized. Marx epistemology holds that the appeal for higher loyalties is like an escapist way of dealing with the conflicting realities of social life. Conflict theory does emphasize the need for humanistic approach in confronting social interpretation.

5.18 Feminist Integrated Theories.

This theory examines how the women have been marginalized, stereotyped or ignored in the criminological discourse. The theorists here try to explain crime from a gender perspective with a major aim being to revamp the lack of attention given to women in the study of crime. Thus it does not have its own concrete postulations but does draw from the other theories.

6.0 INTRODUCTION TO CORRECTIONAL DEBATE

All theories aim to have a utility value. Theories explain phenomenon or provide basis for action. In the preceding section we took an overview of the criminological theories. All that these theories try to do is to provide the best platform for evolution of programs that can work in crime management and prevention. After understanding crime in all its probable causes, society finds it needful to correct or anticipate it and thus prevent it. Society then tries to find best possible ways to correct a criminal and empower such a criminal to refrain from reoffending. This urge has produced another form of debate, the corrective and or rehabilitation debate. The basic quest for this discourse is to determine what works and how it works. Understanding crime, how it occurs and how it affects the society propels one into the quest for program models and rationalization of their impact.

In this section, we take an overview of the main thrust in the corrective debate. Corrective measures are prescriptions by the protagonists of the corrective systems-the scholars, magistrates, judges and jury. Totality of judicial system is looked upon by the society as the main determinant of how the criminals are to be dealt with. Prescription of sentences could therefore be considered as the beginning of the corrective system. The burden of correction however lies not with the judicial system, but with institutions such as prisons and the non-custodial sentence agencies (probation, community service agencies, other penal systems).

The problem of crime has always enlisted the need to find its remedy mainly propelled by the undesirable nature of the outcome of crime. The "undesirable" in this case being a social interpretation of the behavior. Correction of criminal behavior refers to "both programs and agencies that have legal authority for the custody and supervision of offenders convicted of crime (Tony Ward†*, T. G.) (Kinyanjui, 2008). According to scholars, the term itself brings out the thrust of corrective services. Thus, correction services hopes to make offenders come to recognition that their behavior is antisocial and motivate them to change their behavior so that it becomes more beneficial to the society and perhaps their own goals. This view of correction services emphasizes the need for the services to have both the individual benefit and the social value. As a result, the question that begs to be addressed is how best can this be achieved?

6.1 Restorative Justice

There are different approaches that have been advocated to achieve the best results in crime management. Those who view crime from a social perspective, prescribe corrective measures that have a social bearing. In this regard programs and policies in place tend to recognize society as central in any corrective initiatives. On the other hand those who consider crime to be entirely an individual's responsibility tend to focus on correction from a personalized view, more like a doctor patient relationship. Scholars have also argued that corrective services are part of restorative justice. Restorative justice has its main goal as enabling the offenders to be law abiding while at the same time enabling those that have offended to regain their self worth. (Kinyanjui, 2008)

Restorative justice is a broad area that has been used for a long time through the customary practice. The handbook (United Nations) for restorative justice developed by the UNODC gives the most comprehensive coverage of the theme. In her doctoral thesis, Sarah Muringa Kinyanjui LL.B, 2008, affirms that in the Kenyan context, restorative justice has very strong in the different cultures of the people of Kenya. She has illustrated how different communities approached the issue.

The main objective of this treatment is to achieve a situation where the offender becomes a full functioning member of society beyond the offence. The plans have elements of rehabilitation and reintegration. It has the following broad objectives that guide the formulation and implementation of the programs:

- Restore community order and peace and repair damaged relationships
- Denounce criminal behavior as unacceptable and reaffirm community values
- Support victims, give them a voice, enable their participation and address their needs
- Encouraging all concerned parties to take responsibility, particularly by the offenders
- Identify restorative, forward looking outcomes
- Prevent recidivism by encouraging change in individual offenders and facilitating their reintegration into the community (United Nations)

The objectives do emphasis a process that should be followed in the practice of the restorative justice. The process begins with the individual, to the victim and finally to the entire community. The goal of the process is to harness all the available resources in enabling the offender to become a full functioning member of the community and thereby avoid recidivism. In essence its success depends on the assumptions that there is:

    (a) an identifiable victim;
    (b) voluntary participation by the victim;
    (c) an offender who accepts responsibility for his/her criminal behavior; and,
    (d) non-coerced participation of the offender.

These assumptions become the basis on which efforts for restoration are made. If the offender fulfills the above assumptions the victim must on the other hand be willing to participate in the process.

The creativity of the corrective agencies determines the success of the process. Literature indicates that where it has been practiced successfully the reward for the treatment of offences has been scaled up because of its detailed nature and inclusiveness. The fact that it has relied on the cultures and the traditions of different community set up contribute to its success. Rather than give prescribed way of achieving restorative justice, the thrust is in the use its objectives and principles (United Nations)Thus, it asserts that treatment of offenders should take a broad view.

6.2 Treatment Plans

As a result of this fact, there is no agreement as to what works in realizing the intended goals. A document posted on UNDOC website captures this reality, "the issue of offender rehabilitation is a controversial and contested one. The flashpoints include debate over the effectiveness of rehabilitation and the view that, even if treatment does reduce reoffending, offenders do not deserve the opportunity to learn new skills and ultimately a chance at better lives. Instead, the argument goes, they should be humanely contained and the focus of sentencing should be on retribution rather than treatment (Garland, 2001)"

(Tony Ward†*, T. G.). This concern brings into debate the purpose of the treatment plans and their efficacy. Corrective debate thrusts around this fact. Do we treat people that have wronged others, or should we make them to pay (retribution) for their acts? Informed by the human rights doctrine and decrees agreed upon by countries through United Nations, there is a view that offender treatment should be viewed more positively. The debate is skewed towards the fact that rehabilitation and restoration is better than retribution.

The above quoted study reviews what works in the treatment of offenders and what doesn't. It reviews three specific models for offenders" treatment. The model uses sex offenders to show the different treatment models:

a) Risk Need Rensposivity model (RNR)
b) Good life Model
c) Self-Regulation model (Canada), (Tony Ward†*, T. G.)

6.2.1 Risk need Rensposivity model

What this study does is to take the debate on rehabilitation and treatment plans debate into a higher analytical level. For one, it suggests that treatments plans that work begin at a point where the offenders are classified. It suggests that there are high risk and low risk offenders. It implies that not all offences can be treated using treatment plans. The study notes that the risk principle suggests that offenders assessed as being at higher risk for offending should receive higher levels of intervention, including high intensity treatment, than offenders who are at lower risk (Canada)

Not all offences can be effectively treated using treatment plans. Thus to some extent the plans should be discriminatory. Discrimination is for the purposes of reducing efforts that would end up not being measured. It suggests that by focusing on high risk offenders it will be possible to identify the factors that aggravate crime commission. The thrust of the argument is that high risk offenders have an element of cognitive behavior usually exhibited before the commission of the offence. It is this factor that should be explored in the entire treatment process.

On the other hand, "the need principle proposes that only those factors empirically associated with criminal behavior should be targeted in treatment, since targeting these factors for change is most likely to be associated with reductions in recidivism" (Tony Ward†*, T. G.) Thus in treatment the real goal and fear is the fact the offender may go back to the offence, thus rendering the process ineffective. But by focusing on this principle, the treatment plans then become specific. It advocates for an empirical and testable approach. The offenders' needs are both varied and some are far beyond the reach of those drawing treatment plans. Attempting to address all are needs would lead to the burn out of officers and more so make it impossible to measure any success or failure of any particular approach.

It also proposes while focusing on the needs of the offender, there should be a distinction between what is static and what is dynamic. According to this study, the treatment plans should target the dynamic needs because they inform behavior. The dynamic needs constitute the criminogenic needs of the offenders. They have to do with attitudes, motives, and the aggravating factors that can be addressed by the treatment planner. These can be measured and altered. Static needs constitute the non-criminogenic needs. They do not influence the behavior of the offender.

In the analysis of the responsivity, the study asserts that "the responsivity principle represents the interaction between treatment and the individual, and states that correctional programmes should be matched to offenders' learning styles, level of motivations, culture, and personal and interpersonal circumstances" (Tony Ward†*, T. G.) This completes the RNR model.

The importance of this is that it integrates the risks and needs. It brings the importance of considering the offender's resources in determining what works. The need for this consideration is the linkage it provides between the offender, the treatment planner and the community. The offender has the prospects of following what he can be able to conceive in his/her cognitive faculties. There is more prospects in keeping that than what is hard to grasp and follow. Thus, focus on what the offender can learn easily and keep in correcting the offender. It also notes that the way the offender responds to a treatment model will be determined by the baggage he /she carries in form of culture, social environment and socialization. The task here in drawing the treatment plans is to identify what the offender will respond to aided by cultures and social environment.

Reviewing this model shows that it borrows heavily from the cognitive behavioral theory and approaches. It advocates on what can be observed, measured and manipulated. It advocates the consideration of the interaction of the offender, victim and the community. Indeed, the scholars argue that this has been the single factor towards the success of the model in the formulation of the treatment plans. The challenge is therefore to come up with programs that will take into consideration as much as possible the principles of this model.

6.2.2 Good life model:

This model is a critique of the above model. It argues that the RNR model focuses on the negative aspects of the offender. It argues that RNR assumes that the offenders are not capable of having positive attributes. Good Life Model assumes that it is possible to tap the positive aspects of the offenders in drawing of treatment plans. It asserts "more specifically, offenders are seen as psychological agents who seek to live meaningful, satisfactory, and worthwhile lives. The fact that they fail to do this suggests that there are problems in the ways they are seeking human goods — problems embodying a number of flaws in their good lives plans (i.e., inappropriate means, lack of scope, incoherence or conflict, and lack of capacity)" (Tony Ward†*, T. G.)

By recognizing that the offender is not inherently a „bad person" it builds confidence with the said offender. It humanizes the offender in line with Tokyo rules (United Nations), (United Nations) emphasize offenders human rights should be respected. This model then challenges the treatment planners to search for strengths within the offenders. It encourages the treatment officers to identify the offender's personality traits that the treatment officer can use to motivate the offender to overcome the weaknesses that lead him/her to commit the offence. It therefore challenges the treatment worker to listen to the offender's unspoken language with an aim of identifying what can be used to achieve restoration for the offender.

A review of this model shows that it has to use a lot of psychology in the line of treatment. This is because, it requires special skills to analyze the offender in order to discover the positives within them. In absence of the specialized skills, it is important to have a basic understanding of the theoretical explanations that can be relied upon.

6.2.3 Self-regulation model:

This model is inside looking. It involves working with

the offenders to recognize the paths they used to end up being offenders. It suggests that the offender is actively involved in the crime commission and through a conscious process it is possible to come up with a workable treatment plan. The study uses the sexual offenders to illustrate how this model works.

The salient feature of this model is the suggestion that the offender goes through a process of analysis, planning and execution of an offence. In so doing, the offender goes through a nine phase process in commission of a crime and its justification. In brief, the nine phases are summarized as:

The individual experiences a life event that triggers an appraisal of the event based on existing cognitive schema, goals, needs, and implicit theories. (PHASE 1)

The appraisal of the life event triggers the desire for offending or for behaviors associated with offending

(PHASE 2)

The individual establishes an offence-related goal

(PHASE 3)

Pre-offence behaviors that are likely to lead offence are exhibited. (negative expectations may be translated to positive offence behaviors).

(PHASE 6)

The individual evaluates this situation in light of offence-related goals and the expected effectiveness of strategies selected to achieve these goals-and chooses a pathway to commit crime

(PHASE 5)

The individual selects the strategy that will achieve his goal to either avoid offending or to approach offending (PHASE 4)

Individuals' perceptions of the victims of their offences are related to distinct goals with respect to offending.

(PHASE 7)

(PHASE 8)
Post-offence phases-individuals evaluate their behavior immediately following the offence (and may be develop intentions and expectations with respect to future offending)

Dealing with aftermath of offending.

(PHASE 9)

Adapted from (Tony Ward†*, T. G.)

The above nine phases were developed using the sexual offenders. The offence used has a victim. In drawing up the phases, the scholars identified four main pathways the offender use to commit offences. The four pathways determine how the offender controls himself from committing the crime or in dealing with the consequences of the offence. Depending on the pathway, the self-regulation is effective or weak. The following is the summary of the pathways and the self-regulation option adopted:

Pathway	Regulatory Style	Description
Avoidance-passive	Under-regulation	Desire to avoid offending but lacking the coping skills to prevent it from happening
Avoidance-active	Mis-regulation	Direct attempt to control deviant thought and fantasies but use of ineffective or counterproductive strategies

Approach-automatic	Under-regulation	Direct attempt to control deviant thought and fantasies but use of ineffective or counterproductive strategies
Approach-explicit	Effective-regulation	Desire to offend and the use of careful planning to execute offences; harmful goals concerning offending

Adapted from: (Tony Ward†*, T. G.)

In coming up with treatment plan, the goal in this model is to take note of where the offender is in terms of explaining the offence or ability to avoid the future offending. The pathway gives the cognitive interpretation of the offence while the regulation deals with the attempts of the offender to justify (either positively or negatively) the commission of the offence.

The model suggests that the offender is usually in a state of internal analysis of intended offence and negotiation of the possible outcomes of the offence. Offenders that tend to view the outcomes as serious, they will attempt to avoid them. The success of this attempt will determine whether they are going to be repeat offenders or not. The offender that high sense of outcomes and that agrees that offence is undesirable both at personal level and at a communal level will tend to avoid the offence altogether, thus quit the life of crime. However, it is possible that he/she will analyze the outcome and justify why it should be committed again. Thus become a repeat offender.

The model advocates that after establishing the internal environment of the offender, treatment plans should use the RNR model discussed above. The model gives the prospects of understanding the offender much better before drawing up the treatment plan. The model seems to work best where the offence involves a victim. From its presentation, it implies that the final phase of the offender where he/she deals with consequences of the offences is of most importance to the treatment worker. At this time the offender is either incarcerated or in a state of psychological trauma.

7.0 LINKAGES BETWEEN THEORIES AND PRACTICE

Probation, community service and aftercare are ways of dealing with an offender. The basis of the services is the belief that locking everybody in the penal institution would not cure the society of crime and neither will it be possible to eliminate all the offenders. The options also affirm that human beings and the society do hold the key to the prevention and management of the offenders. Thus, rather than focusing on the offence the, these methods focus on the individual.

It is therefore imperative to draw linkages between the theories and actual practice. In drawing up these linkages it is important to explore the core basis for non-instutionalization of offenders. In Kenya, just as in the rest of the world, the basis for the non-custodial sentences is the acts of parliament. These acts are the basic infrastructure that enables the services to be executed. In turn the acts of parliament are informed by the international standards as prescribed and agreed upon by United Nations and other international human rights bodies.

Kenya non-custodial services heavily borrows from the Tokyo Rules or the United Nations Minimum Rules for Non-Custodial services. The rules as found in the United Nations Office Of High Commission for Human Rights are included in this book. These rules were informed by some important theories and thinking. Since they form the basis for international law and practice of non-custodial sentences, it is important to draw the salient features that can be deduced.

The following key features are evident in the rules:

- **Respect for humanity:** From the outset, the rules declare that the offender is a human being who should be treated with dignity. As such, the recognition seem to draw a sharp distinction between the offender and the offence. Just like some theories do suggest that the individual is not to be blamed, inherently the human being is actually good. This assertion does also imply that efforts should be geared towards the factors that lead one to offend.

- **Social responsibility in crime management:** The burden of prevention of crime and its management is placed upon the individual and the society. Thus, the offender is to be rehabilitated in a community where he/she comes from. This is closely linked to the theories that state that the criminal is a product of a society. Thus only the same society can then be able to cleanse the "crime" in the person. By being encouraged to promote a sense of responsibility among offenders, the rules do imply that society fails in the first place to play it rightful role as far as crime management is concerned. The rules suggest that perhaps the socialization process did not achieve the necessary results. Thus the community should then be blamed in as far as the individual is to be blamed.

- **Uniqueness of the social set up:** This feature provide for the universality of the application of the rules. The rules recognize that humanity despite the different racial background, social economic set ups, the basic ideals are the same. Thus, the feature dispels any existence of some super human races or minor human races. The rules seem to rebuff the myth that there are some societies that are still evolving and others are at an advanced stage. Instead, the rules do recognize uniqueness of different social set-ups. Human dignity is universal and thus the basics of life including the right to life is the same. In crime management and prevention this feature enables the programs to follow some commonalities but at the same time be specific to particular cultural backgrounds and realities.

- **Goal of crime management:** The rules sets out the goal of crime management as meeting the "rehabilitative needs of the offender, the protection of society and the interests of the victim" This could mean that crime is bound to happen hence the admission that the criminal has to be rehabilitated, while the same offender must be restrained from hurting the community. Where the victims are involved their wishes and interests are to be considered. Successful crime management programs „must eradicate criminality" in an individual to make the society feel safe, while at the same time ensuring the offender"s inherent being is protected.

- **Role of human rights:** The rules state in clear terms that the human rights of the offender are to be respected. Despite being an offender, the person is not stripped of
  the humanity by the nature of the offence. This seems to be informed by theories that do suggest the crime committed can be used to describe the personality of a person. Rather, the crime is just an isolated act in a broad spectrum of possible behavioral tendencies. Sort, do not entirely blame individuals, but investigate to know what caused the crime and treat it.

- **De-stigmatization:** This is expressed by the emphasis that the trend should be towards depenalization. One of the greatest criticism of the penal system is that it breeds hard core criminals. Thus, all efforts are to be made to avoid it. There is evidence that rehabilitation without penalization has better prospects. Care should then be taken to ensure that what penalization does is not found in the non-custodial sentence.

- **Non-discrimination:** Discrimination is one that increases stigmatization. Hence the rules do advocate against discrimination. Non-custodial officers and enforcers are therefore obliged to be on the lookout against anything that can accelerates discrimination. This is perhaps based on the labeling theories. As seen earlier, efforts should be made not to brand offenders but that they should be appreciated as human beings.

- **Place of crime management:** Rules emphasize that crime management should be emphasized. Crime is to be managed as a factor of humanity that can be isolated
  from the individual. It implies that using appropriate treatment plans, criminality in an individual can be addressed. Again, theories that consider criminality as a pathological problem influence this rule. The treatment plans are to the non-custodial officers what proper clinical therapy is to a medical doctor. What this implies is that treatment plans must attempt to address the real problems and curb the crime from continuing to happen.

- **Philosophy of non-custodial services:** The philosophy of the non-custodial sentencing rules according to the UN seems to be that the offenders cannot be discarded because of their offences. They still remain human beings capable of living better and fruitful lives given a chance. Reading the rules, the theme of considering the offender as a person is implied in almost every phrase. Thus, the rules are heavily human centered recognizing the individual as capable of having the best of life beyond the offence.

- **Determination of non-custodial sentence beneficiaries:** The rules also give general guidelines on those to benefit. First offenders, juveniles and young persons are to be considered for non-custodial sentencing. The rules do give guidelines for those in the justice system to have an idea how they can make use of the option.

Probation officers need to have an understanding of these rules and these salient features. The utility of this is that it will be possible for the practitioners to realize that theories do inform practice. Most important is to understand what interventions can work in a given situation guided by these international standards.

8.0 UNDERSTANDING THE PRACTICE IN KENYAN CONTEXT

Having browsed through theories and standards in the practice on the non-custodial sentencing, the next big question is where are we as a nation in terms of the practice of the non-custodial service delivery? Probation service has been in Kenya since pre-independence having been introduced by the colonial government. Its existence in the country has been firm yet not pronounced remaining as a less publicized public service.

Despite this fact, its impact has been felt and has made its practice to endure. Great efforts have been done by both the government through legislation and the department to ensure that the service actually gains its rightful recognition. Courts have all along relied upon the probation department to execute its mandate.

Over the last few years however, the government has been going through major reforms in all sectors. All government departments are then called upon to state their case as to how relevant they are in solving the problems faced by the public. Coupled with the desire of the country to achieve Vision 2030, the ambitious blue print for economic, social and political development, it is imperative that creativity be brought in all sectors to contribute to this dream.

As a department, the greatest impetus towards the change and improvement comes from the government's realization that it needs to efficiently deliver services. One way has been through the reduction of cost of service delivery and targeting the growth sectors. The department is then key in ensuring that the goal is achieved through the prison decongestion programme. Studies both locally and outside the country have shown that it is far more expensive to rehabilitate one custodial offender than it is to rehabilitate a non-custodial one . The savings computed during the evaluation of work done by the non-custodial offenders should not only be figures but should for instance be used to deliver a case of the realization of the part of the government goals.

The burden of making the department even more relevant, lays not with the government legislations, but more so with ability of the officers on the ground to show that they can deliver and that they can contribute towards realization of better growth of the department. To do this, practitioners must first embrace the challenges that they face. Studies world over have shown that not a single country has executed the non-custodial services without challenges. It is not unique to Kenya for instance that:

- Officers in the field lack adequate transport facilities.

- The department is underfunded by the central government-which incidentally remain the main funder in many countries.
- That officer is overwhelmed by case work, often ending doing only case work and not doing rehabilitation.
- That cultural barrier hinders effective service delivery.
- That the offenders recidivism remain the single most important challenges in the field of non-custodial services.
- That record keeping is a big issue.

Despite these challenges, efforts have been made by the other nations to go beyond the challenges and creatively come up with workable solutions for the effective service delivery. The department has huge amount of data both at the station levels and the national level that can be used to assist in overcoming some of the challenges.

To understand how non-custodial services can be improved begins at appreciation of what is expected of the practitioners. The non-custodial officer is not only a case worker, but has to double up as a critical thinker too. Reflections on the field experiences would yield insights into what could be the best practices. Currently efforts are being made to ensure that the field work is adequately documented, stored and analysed. To do this, the officers on the ground need to embrace the art of data gathering, compilation and analysis. Accurately gathered data can give pointers to the bigger picture. If the department successfully implements its vision of enabling specialization in different areas of non-custodial services, then officers will be more challenged to be constructive and creative. They will be more challenged to constructively interpret the data in a more a detailed manner.

Beyond the common logistical challenges therefore, the critical challenge that has to be embraced is that of professionalism. What for instance constitute professionalism among non-custodial officers? Is a non-custodial officer concerned primarily with the writing social inquiries, presenting them to court, supervising the court orders or is it more than that? Despite being the core duties of the non-custodial officers, they are not adequate by themselves. What these core duties do is to provide a mine of information, data and experiences that can be used to propel the department to greater heights and also enable the society interrogates what it goes through and especially how to deal with the problem of crime. The data should be useful in drawing up possible criminogenic needs imputed by the gathered data.

Kenya's cultural background is quite diverse. This diversity informs the approaches that have to be adopted. In her doctoral thesis that addressed restorative justice, focusing on juvenile justice in Kenya, (Kinyanjui, 2008)notes that each culture had its own way of dealing with the problem of crime. She notes that communities had unique ways of ensuring that restorative justice was achieved and that somehow the problem of crime was addressed. The means achieved both restorative and deterrence objectives. But this factor brings the real challenge in the practice of non-custodial practice. For instance, can the approaches used by a community in Nyanza be the same as that used on North Eastern, or among the Coastal communities? Or better put, can the approaches used in the Nyanza be applied with the same level of success in Central Province? If not, is there a working model that can be used in all cultural diversity with the considerable level of success? It is not enough to accept that gun crime is petty in North Eastern but a serious offence in Nairobi Province. One has got to interrogate the meaning of the same offence being given different meanings within the same jurisdiction.

Beyond the interrogation, there should be attempts to come up with common working assessment tools. Presently, Probation department encourages officers to come up with treatment plans for the various offences. Treatment plans are bound to be numerous and haphazard if foregoing interrogation is not done. For instance, can the treatment plan crafted in Eastern

Province be used among offenders in Tana River and achieve the same results? It might be not possible. Before the treatment plan is done, attempts should be made to ensure the tool used to come up with a decision to use a certain treatment plan is adequately considered. A comprehensive assessment tool needs to be developed. The process of developing the assessment tool should involve all the officers.

Exploring the practice of non-custodial services practice in Kenya should be considered creatively. Without waiting for funded research, there should be attempts to understand whether the data already collected over the years make any sense. The following could be worth considering:

- Do we have crime typologies in the country or in other words, does crime take similar patterns?
- Is it possible to evaluate field interventions to understand lessons implied?
- Can the data in the field, the interventions that works breed new knowledge in making a common assessment/decision making tool?
- Is it possible to treat similar crimes using similar treatment plans across the culturally diverse geographical areas? If not, what is implication?

Probation department in present day is much advanced than it is used to be about five years or ten years ago. For one, the profession is staffed with officers with great zeal and potential. The advantage is that the officers will have to compete for the better of service delivery. Competition breeds improvement and innovation.

Working environment has been comparatively improved. It is now possible to find computers and tools of trade in the variously well constructed offices. A look at development funding in the department shows considerable resources have dedicated towards improvement of the working environment. Within a short time, the department will go live with modern data management system. This will provide new challenges to the officers.

9.0 WAY FORWARD

Probation practice in Kenya today is both interesting and challenging. Interesting because, the department is going through a moment of rapid changes. Staffing enhancement, technological changes and more critical analysis of the practice amidst the new social challenges are among the interesting factors at play. The periodic five years strategic plan for the department charts the way forward and gives direction into the future. Importantly, this document can inspire innovation at the individual level to accelerate probation practice to higher heights.

It is imperative that the officer be adequately prepared to ensure that the theoretical basis of the non-custodial practice is not pushed to the periphery. Innovation calls on the innovator to visit the archive and discover the hidden treasures. The future of non-custodial service lies in the ability of the practitioners to integrate theories and practical solutions aided by the technology. The challenge is real because coming across works that are specific to the African context let alone Kenya in the internet is a daunting task. It is possible to reverse this trend and make use of the technology for the benefit of the service delivery.

Technology need not be seen as inhibitive but should

be used creatively to come up with solutions that are sound, based on the theoretical framework and that are implementable. For instance, as we focus on development of treatment plans that work, there will be need to first be able to appraise the entire nation's collected data and understand what criminogenic needs are common in given offences. May be certain offences no matter where they are committed have given crimonogenic needs. By use of technology, the data already gathered can be analyzed and this fact can be tested whether true or not.

It would be possible to draw treatment plans if it was established through empirical data that certain offences arise out of given criminogenic needs. But this would not be possible without first of all coming up with an effective assessment tool. An assessment tool that can be universally used and give universal results would lead us to understand what treatment plan to use when and where.

Assessment tools developed through collaboration with all stakeholders need to be implemented and evaluated. The arresting officers, the prosecutors, the judges/magistrates and jury can make use of the assessments to achieve impact in the correction business. This is because the tool would make all the stakeholders refocus on what makes them do what they do. To the non-custodial officers such a process can assist address the old challenge-recidivism.

Social inquiry remains one of the single most important tool for a probation officer. Through it, the officer can document and use it for analysis of criminogenic needs, the aggravating factors and the crime environment. However, its effectiveness and indeed of all other tools is hinged on the officer's thorough understanding of the theoretical framework that inform Probation practice. This command will enable the officer to ask the right questions.

For instance, can it enable the officer to capture the risk of recidivism before it occurs? Can the report and the other tools make it possible to establish whether a certain criminogenic factor would lead to recidivism whether the offence occurs in North Eastern or Nairobi? These questions arise out of the fact that the courts need to make decisions within a given time and there may not have time to read a detailed and lengthy social inquiry report.

Apart from the tools, there will be need to come up with workable partnerships with the community. In the practice of non-custodial services, the community all over seems to be faced by the challenge getting the needed community support. Community support should be in the form of community members embracing those committed to non-custodial sentence. The Tokyo Rules or the UN Minimum rules of Non-custodial sentence[67] do emphasize the need for community support. Community is seen as the most important factor in the success of the non-custodial sentence.

Partnerships should aim at coming up with projects that endure with time and that involve the offenders to the maximum. Examples of youth involvement programs include a program that the writer implemented in Tana River in the year 2011. The program implementation was anchored on the Probation Cases Committee which had the following objectives:

- Bring to the attention of young people contents of sexual offences act.
- Minimize and eventually eradicate cases of children under the age of 18 years being charged with defilement.
- Enhance rights awareness in light of sexual offences act.

The project was implemented in the community with the community being the main driver of the program. The following was its implementation model:

- There was a football competition that brought

together community youth groups and we had twelve teams in total that brought together over one hundred and fifty team members.

- Commentators used the sexual offences act 2006 as reference materials focusing on offences and sentences that are prescribed.
- There was a talent show, where the youths and community members performed drama, music, skits, poems and narratives around the theme of sexual offences act.
- An expert was invited to comment on the Sexual Offences act at the end of all the presentations and
- Judges picked the best items for awards

There were vital lessons learned during the implementation of the project in Tana River. These were:

- Empower the youth to fight and prevent crime: Youth told stories in language they understood, articulated the theme better than any conference could do.
- Youths have talents that go beyond education levels: Ordinary youths presented creative items that passed a message despite education standards.
- Networking in project implementation adds value.

- In service delivery, the community does not have to demand for services-we could attract support from civil society to enable us reach out to the community to create necessary rapport with it for sustainability.

This example depends so much on how a practitioners will forge the partnership. There would be need for willingness to try new initiatives all the time and be willingness to start all over again in case of failure.

Use of voluntary probation officers needs to be evaluated in terms of whether it meets the expectation of the department, whether it could be improved or whether there are other ways it could be utilized. Could for instance the youth groups in the community be incorporated in the voluntary probation officers program? May be they should be corporate partnerships such that community groups be brought into the program instead of individuals or in addition to them.

ANNEXURE

United Nations Standard Minimum Rules for Non-custodial Measures (The Tokyo Rules)

•

Adopted by General Assembly resolution 45/110 of 14 December 1990

I. General principles

1. Fundamental aims

1.1 The present Standard Minimum Rules provide a set of basic principles to promote the use of non-custodial measures, as well as minimum safeguards for persons subject to alternatives to imprisonment.

1.2 The Rules are intended to promote greater community involvement in the management of criminal justice, specifically in the treatment of offenders, as well as to promote among offenders a sense of responsibility towards society.

1.3 The Rules shall be implemented taking into account the political, economic, social and cultural conditions of each country and the aims and objectives of its criminal justice system.

1.4 When implementing the Rules, Member States shall endeavour to ensure a proper balance between the rights of individual offenders, the rights of victims, and the concern of society for public safety and crime prevention.

1.5 Member States shall develop non-custodial measures within their legal systems to provide other options, thus reducing the use of imprisonment, and to rationalize criminal justice policies, taking into account the observance of human rights, the requirements of social justice and the rehabilitation needs of the offender.

2. The scope of non-custodial measures

2.1 The relevant provisions of the present Rules shall be applied to all persons subject to prosecution, trial or the execution of a

sentence, at all stages of the administration of criminal justice. For the purposes of the Rules, these persons are referred to as "offenders", irrespective of whether they are suspected, accused or sentenced.

2.2 The Rules shall be applied without any discrimination on the grounds of race, colour, sex, age, language, religion, political or other opinion, national or social origin, property, birth or other status.

2.3 In order to provide greater flexibility consistent with the nature and gravity of the offence, with the personality and background of the offender and with the protection of society and to avoid unnecessary use of imprisonment, the criminal justice system should provide a wide range of non-custodial measures, from pre-trial to post-sentencing dispositions. The number and types of non-custodial measures available should be determined in such a way so that consistent sentencing remains possible.

2.4 The development of new non-custodial measures should be encouraged and closely monitored and their use systematically evaluated.

2.5 Consideration shall be given to dealing with offenders in the community avoiding as far as possible resort to formal proceedings or trial by a court, in accordance with legal safeguards and the rule of law.

2.6 Non-custodial measures should be used in accordance with the principle of minimum intervention.

2.7 The use of non-custodial measures should be part of

the movement towards depenalization and decriminalization instead of interfering with or delaying efforts in that direction.

3 . Legal safeguards

3.1 The introduction, definition and application of non-custodial measures shall be prescribed by law.

3.2 The selection of a non-custodial measure shall be based on an assessment of established criteria in respect of both the nature and gravity of the offence and the personality, background of the offender, the purposes of sentencing and the rights of victims.

3.3 Discretion by the judicial or other competent independent authority shall be exercised at all stages of the proceedings by ensuring full accountability and only in accordance with the rule of law.

3.4 Non-custodial measures imposing an obligation on the offender, applied before or instead of formal proceedings or trial , shall require the offender's consent.

3.5 Decisions on the imposition of non-custodial measures shall be subject to review by a judicial or other competent independent authority, upon application by the offender.

3.6 The offender shall be entitled to make a request or complaint to a judicial or other competent independent authority on matters affecting his or her individual rights in the implementation of non-custodial measures.

3.7 Appropriate machinery shall be provided for the recourse and, if possible, redress of any grievance related to non-compliance with internationally recognized human rights.

3.8 Non-custodial measures shall not involve medical or psychological experimentation on, or undue risk of physical or mental injury to, the offender.

3.9 The dignity of the offender subject to non-custodial measures shall be protected at all times.

3.10 In the implementation of non-custodial measures, the offender's rights shall not be restricted further than was authorized by the competent authority that rendered the original decision.

3.11 In the application of non-custodial measures, the offender's right to privacy shall be respected, as shall be the right to privacy of the offender's family.

3.12 The offender's personal records shall be kept strictly confidential and closed to third parties. Access to such records shall be limited to persons directly concerned with the disposition of the offender's case or to other duly authorized persons.

4 . Saving clause

4.1 Nothing in these Rules shall be interpreted as precluding the application of the Standard Minimum Rules for the Treatment of Prisoners, the United Nations Standard Minimum Rules for the Administration of Juvenile Justice, the Body of Principles for the Protection of All Persons under Any Form of Detention or Imprisonment or any other human rights instruments and standards recognized by the international community and relating to the treatment of offenders and the protection of their basic human rights.

II. Pre-trial stage

5. Pre-trial dispositions

5.1 Where appropriate and compatible with the legal system, the police, the prosecution service or other agencies dealing with criminal cases should be empowered to discharge the offender if they consider that it is not necessary to proceed with the case for the protection of society, crime prevention or the promotion of respect for the law and the rights of victims. For the purpose of deciding upon the appropriateness of discharge or determination of proceedings, a set of established criteria shall be developed within each legal system. For minor cases the prosecutor may impose suitable non-custodial measures, as appropriate.

6. Avoidance of pre-trial detention

6.1 Pre-trial detention shall be used as a means of last

resort in criminal proceedings, with due regard for the investigation of the alleged offence and for the protection of society and the victim.

6.2 Alternatives to pre-trial detention shall be employed at as early a stage as possible. Pre-trial detention shall last no longer than necessary to achieve the objectives stated under rule 5.1 and shall be administered humanely and with respect for the inherent dignity of human beings.

6.3 The offender shall have the right to appeal to a judicial or other competent independent authority in cases where pre-trial detention is employed.

III. Trial and sentencing stage 7. Social inquiry reports

7.1 If the possibility of social inquiry reports exists, the judicial authority may avail itself of a report prepared by a competent, authorized official or agency. The report should contain social information on the offender that is relevant to the person's pattern of offending and current offences. It should also contain information and recommendations that are relevant to the sentencing procedure. The report shall be factual, objective and unbiased, with any expression of opinion clearly identified.

8. Sentencing dispositions

8.1 The judicial authority, having at its disposal a range of non-custodial measures, should take into consideration in making its decision the rehabilitative needs of the offender, the protection of society and the interests of the victim, who should be consulted whenever appropriate.

8.2 Sentencing authorities may dispose of cases in the following ways:

(a) Verbal sanctions, such as admonition, reprimand and warning; (

b) Conditional discharge;

(c) Status penalties;

(d) Economic sanctions and monetary penalties, such as fines and day-fines;

(e) Confiscation or an expropriation order;

(f) Restitution to the victim or a compensation order;

(g) Suspended or deferred sentence;

(h) Probation and judicial supervision;

(i) A community service order;

(j) Referral to an attendance centre;

(k) House arrest;

(l) Any other mode of non-institutional treatment;

(m) Some combination of the measures listed above.

IV. Post-sentencing stage

9 . Post-sentencing dispositions

9.1 The competent authority shall have at its disposal a wide range of post-sentencing alternatives in order to avoid institutionalization and to assist offenders in their early reintegration into society.

9.2 Post-sentencing dispositions may include:

(a) Furlough and half-way houses;

(b) Work or education release;

(c) Various forms of parole;

(d) Remission;

(e) Pardon.

9.3 The decision on post-sentencing dispositions, except in the case of pardon, shall be subject to review by a judicial or other competent independent authority, upon application of the offender.

9.4 Any form of release from an institution to a non-custodial programme shall be considered at the earliest possible stage.

V. Implementation of non-custodial measures 10. Supervision

10.1 The purpose of supervision is to reduce reoffending and to assist the offender's integration into society in a way which minimizes the likelihood of a return to crime.

10.2 If a non-custodial measure entails supervision, the latter shall be carried out by a competent authority under the specific conditions prescribed by law.

10.3 Within the framework of a given non-custodial measure, the most suitable type of supervision and treatment should be determined for each individual case aimed at assisting the offender to work on his or her offending. Supervision and treatment should be periodically reviewed and adjusted as necessary.

10.4 Offenders should, when needed, be provided with psychological, social and material assistanceand with opportunities to strengthen links with the community and facilitate their reintegration into society.

11 . Duration

11.1 The duration of a non-custodial measure shall not exceed the period established by the competent authority in accordance with the law.

11.2 Provision may be made for early termination of the measure if the offender has responded favourably to it.

12. Conditions

12.1 If the competent authority shall determine the conditions to be observed by the offender, it should take into account both the needs of society and the needs and rights of the offender and the victim.

12.2 The conditions to be observed shall be practical, precise and as few as possible, and be aimed at reducing the likelihood of an offender relapsing into criminal behavior and of increasing the offender's chances of social integration, taking into account the needs of the victim.

12.3 At the beginning of the application of a non-custodial measure, the offender shall receive an explanation, orally and in writing, of the conditions governing the application of the measure, including the offender's obligations and rights.

12.4 The conditions may be modified by the competent authority under the established statutory provisions, in accordance with the progress made by the offender.

13. Treatment process

13.1 Within the framework of a given non-custodial measure, in appropriate cases, various schemes, such as case-work, group therapy, residential programmes and the specialized treatment of various categories of offenders, should be developed to meet the needs of offenders more effectively.

13.2 Treatment should be conducted by professionals who have suitable training and practical experience.

13.3 When it is decided that treatment is necessary, efforts should be made to understand the offender's background, personality, aptitude, intelligence, values and, especially, the circumstances leading to the commission of the offence.

13.4 The competent authority may involve the community and social support systems in the application of non-custodial measures.

13.5 Case-load assignments shall be maintained as far as practicable at a manageable level to ensure the effective implementation of treatment programmes.

13.6 For each offender, a case record shall be established and maintained by the competent authority.

14. Discipline and breach of conditions

14.1 A breach of the conditions to be observed by the offender may result in a modification or revocation of the non-custodial measure.

14.2 The modification or revocation of the non-custodial measure shall be made by the competent authority; this shall be done only after a careful examination of the facts adduced by both the supervising officer and the offender.

14.3 The failure of a non-custodial measure should not automatically lead to the imposition of a custodial measure.

14.4 In the event of a modification or revocation of the non-custodial measure, the competent authority shall attempt to establish a suitable alternative non-custodial measure. A sentence of imprisonment may be imposed only in the absence of other suitable alternatives.

14.5 The power to arrest and detain the offender under supervision in cases where there is a breach of the conditions shall be prescribed by law.

14.6 Upon modification or revocation of the non-custodial measure, the offender shall have the right to appeal to a judicial or other competent independent authority.

VI. Staff

15. Recruitment

15.1 There shall be no discrimination in the recruitment of staff on the grounds of race, colour, sex, age, language, religion, political or other opinion, national or social origin, property, birth or other status. The policy regarding staff recruitment should take into consideration national policies of affirmative action and reflect the diversity of the offenders to be supervised.

15.2 Persons appointed to apply non-custodial measures should be personally suitable and, whenever possible, have appropriate professional training and practical experience. Such qualifications shall be clearly specified.

15.3 To secure and retain qualified professional staff, appropriate service status, adequate salary and benefits commensurate with the nature of the work should be ensured and ample opportunities should be provided for professional growth and career development.

16 . Staff training

16.1 The objective of training shall be to make clear to staff their responsibilities with regard to rehabilitating the offender, ensuring the offender's rights and protecting society. Training should also give staff an understanding of the need to cooperate in and coordinate activities with the agencies concerned.

16.2 Before entering duty, staff shall be given training that includes instruction on the nature of non-custodial measures, the purposes of supervision and the various modalities of the application of non-custodial measures.

16.3 After entering duty, staff shall maintain and improve their knowledge and professional capacity by attending in-service training and refresher courses. Adequate facilities shall be made available for that purpose.

VII. Volunteers and other community resources 17. Public participation

17.1 Public participation should be encouraged as it is a major resource and one of the most important factors in improving ties between offenders undergoing non-custodial measures and the family and community. It should complement the efforts of the criminal justice administration.

17.2 Public participation should be regarded as an opportunity for members of the community to contribute to the protection of their society.

18 . Public understanding and cooperation

18.1 Government agencies, the private sector and the general public should be encouraged to support voluntary organizations that promote noncustodial measures.

18.2 Conferences, seminars, symposia and other activities should be regularly organized to stimulate awareness of the need for public participation in the application of non-custodial measures. 18.3 All forms of the mass media should be utilized to help to

create a constructive public attitude, leading to activities conducive to a broader application of non-custodial treatment and the social integration of offenders.

18.4 Every effort should be made to inform the public of the importance of its role in the implementation of non-custodial measures.

Bibliography

Abretcht, A. (n.d.). *Cesare Lombroso*. Retrieved from Journal of Crimal Law and Criminology Volume 1, Issue 2 Article 6: http://scholarlycommons.law.northwestern.edu/jclc?utm_source=scholarlycommons.law.northwestern.edu%2Fjclc%2Fvol1%2Fiss2%2F6&utm_medium=PDF&utm_campaign=PDFCoverPages

Austrarian Capital Territory. (Sept 2002). *Sentencing Review Issues Paper*. Retrieved from Department of Justice and Community Safety: http://www.jcs.act.gov.au/eLibrary/Sentencing%20Review/IssuesPaperSept2002.pdf

Austrarian Institute of Crimonology. (2009). *Criminal Justice System*. Retrieved from http://www.aic.gov.au/criminal_justice_system/resources/aboutcriminology.html

B. J.Preston. (n.d.). *Paper on sentencing for environmental offences*. Retrieved from Law Link: www.lawlink.nsw.gov.au/lawlink/lec/ll_lec.nsf/vwFiles/Sentencing%20-%20New%20York%20...

Brian J. Ostrom, Matthew Kleiman,Randall M. Hansen. (2002). *Offender Risk Assessment*. Retrieved from A National Institute of Justice Partnership Grant: http://vcsc.virginia.gov/risk_off_rpt.pdf

Canada. (n.d.). *Risk Need*. Retrieved from Public Safety: http://www.publicsafety.gc.ca/res/cor/rep/risk_need_200706-eng.aspx

F. Elwell. (n.d.). *Theorists: Durkheim*. Retrieved from Retrieved from Rogers State University:

www.faculty.rsu.edu/~felwell/Theorists/Durkheim/Presentation/Durk heim.pdf

IDEAS. (n.d.). *Improving our Practice of sentencing.* . Retrieved from http://ideas.repec.org/a/cup/utilit/v9y1997i01p99-114_00.html-

Inkeles, A. (1997). *Introduction to Sociology.* Nairobi: Eastern Edition.

International Journal of Criminology. (n.d.). *Restorative Justice.* . Retrieved from International Journal of Crimonology: www.internetjournalofcriminology.com/Mantle,%20Fox%20&%20D hami%20-%20Restorative%20...

Justice, N. I. (n.d.). *Restorative Justice.* Retrieved from www.ojp.usdoj.gov/nij/topics/courts/restorative-justice/welcome.htm

Kinyanjui, S. M. (2008). *A Geneological Analysis of Criminal Justice In Kenya, Rebirth of Restorative Justice for Juveniles?* Retrieved from Doctoral Thesis: https://lra.le.ac.uk/bitstream/2381/4495/1/2008kinyanjuismphdinlaw. pdf

National Insitute of Justice. (n.d.). *Five things about Deterrence.* Retrieved from http://nij.gov/five-things/pages/deterrence.aspx

Richard S Frase. (n.d.). *Comparative Perspectives on Sentencing.* Retrieved from Richwww.rashkind.com/alternatives/dir_14/Frase_Comparative%20Pe rsp ectives%20on%20Sentencing.doc

Spengler. H. E. . (n.d.). *Deutsches Institut für Wirtschaftsforschung.* Retrieved from http://www.diw.de/english/products/publications/discussion_papers/ 2 7539.html

Tibetts, S. G., & Craig, H. (2010). *Criminological Theory.* Carlifornia: Sage Publication.

Tony Ward†*, T. G. (n.d.). *The treatment of offenders: current practice.* Retrieved from United Nations Office Of Drugs : http://www.unodc.org

Twente University. (n.d.). *Cognitive theories.* Retrieved from Retrieved from <http://www.tcw.utwente.nl/

United Nations. (n.d.). *Handbook of basic principles and promising practices on Alternatives to Imprisonment.* Retrieved from Crime: http://www.unodc.org

United Nations. (n.d.). *Handbook on Restorativejustice programmes.* Retrieved from Crime: http://www.unodc.org

United Nations. (2006). *Alternative to Incarceration.* Retrieved from Crime: www.unodc.org/pdf/criminal_justice/ALTERNATIVES_INCARCERATION.pdf

United Nations. (n.d.). *Tokyo Rules.* Retrieved from Office of High Commission for Human Rights. : http://www2.ohchr.org/english/law/tokyorules.htm

United Nations. (n.d.). *United Nations Minimum Non-Custodial Rules-Tokyo Rules.* . Retrieved from http/www.un.org/documents/ga/res/45/a45r110.htm